LEARN TO READ

Phonics Storybook

25 Simple Stories & Activities for Beginner Readers

LAURIN BRAINARD
ILLUSTRATIONS BY LIZZY DOYLE

CALLISTO PUBLISHING

Copyright © 2020 by Callisto Publishing LLC
Cover and internal design © 2020 by Callisto Publishing LLC
Illustrations © 2020 Lizzy Doyle
Art Director: Angela Navarra
Art Producer: Maura Boland
Editor: Jeanine Le Ny
Production Editor: Melissa Edeburn
Production Manager: Holly Haydash

Callisto Publishing and the colophon are registered trademarks of Callisto Publishing LLC

Published by Callisto Publishing LLC C/O Sourcebooks LLC
P.O. Box 4410, Naperville, Illinois 60567-4410
(630) 961-3900
callistopublishing.com

This product conforms to all applicable CPSC and CPSIA standards.

Source of Production: Wing King Tong Paper Products Co.Ltd. Shenzhen, Guangdong Province, China Date of Production: January 2024
Run Number: 5037739

Printed and bound in China.
WKT 15

Contents

Introduction

· ·

Learning phonics is an important skill to master as a new reader. Phonics is a technique that relates specific sounds with letters, or groups of letters, in the alphabet. As a first-grade teacher and mom of preschoolers, I have personally seen and shared in the excitement a child experiences when they first learn to sound out words and begin to read.

The importance of learning to read is why I crafted this treasury of 25 cute stories, featuring many of the word families that your child will need to know to become a confident reader. Word families are groups of words that contain the same ending patterns, such as **cat**, **sat**, and **mat**. The predictable pattern makes it easier for a child to develop reading skills. Strong readers quickly recognize letters and their sound patterns, and a great way to practice word recognition is by seeing the letters and sound patterns in a story. I've also included two activities at the end of each story so that your child can practice identifying the sounds they've just read. Using the words and sounds in activities after reading these stories will help your child remember the words and sounds in the future.

As your child advances through the book, each story will gradually increase in difficulty based on the word families, additional phonetic sounds, or the structure of the sentences. With repeated practice, your child will begin to recognize each of the word family sounds in this book, and then may begin to identify these sounds in other books.

I can't wait for you to see your child's excitement as they travel down the path of reading success!

Note to Parents

Whether your child is not yet reading or is just beginning to read, this book can help them develop reading skills. Each of the first seven stories focuses on one word family. Each family is made up of words that contain a consonant-vowel-consonant sound. Help your child read these words by slowly sounding out the individual sounds and then blending the sounds together. If your child is not yet reading, have them point to the words as you read. Then, talk about other words that might rhyme with the word family.

Once your child can read these initial stories with ease, they will be ready for stories that feature multiple word families or consonant blends (such as the fl-sound in flop). Some stories require more practice than others. You do not need to introduce a new story every day.

Here are some more tips to help you guide your child:

1. Begin each story by showing your child the featured word family and teaching the sound the letters make.
2. Have your child point to each word while reading.
3. If your child struggles with a word, help them sound it out. If a word cannot be sounded out (such as "the"), say it out loud and have your child repeat it.
4. Use your finger to model the activities on the page while your child writes the answers. If your child is in the prewriting stage, have them use one of their fingers to trace and point to the answers.
5. Read as often as your child wants you to! The more you practice these word families, the easier they will become for your child to read and recognize. Young children learn best when the material they are learning is entertaining, so make sure you are prepared to have fun!

My Pet

SKILL FOCUS:
-et word family

My pet is at the vet.

Can the vet help my pet?

"Get the pet wet," said the vet.

All set to help my pet!

Go get the jet.

Do we like the vet? You bet!

Say the words. Then trace the words.

pet   pet   pet   pet

vet   vet   vet   vet

get   get   get   get

wet   wet   wet   wet

set   set   set   set

jet   jet   jet   jet

Activity Time

Complete the maze. Color the circles that have words from the **-et** word family.

jet	pet	vet	get	said	do
can	help	we	vet	wet	like
we	you	the	go	set	my
the	like	my	can	bet	jet
do	go	help	you	at	pet
the	like	it	can	we	vet
do	go	help	you	at	set

The Big Pig

SKILL FOCUS:
-ig word family

Look at the pig.

The pig has a wig.

The pig can do a jig.

The pig likes to dig.

The pig eats figs.

Now the pig is big!

Activity Time

Say the words. Then trace the words.

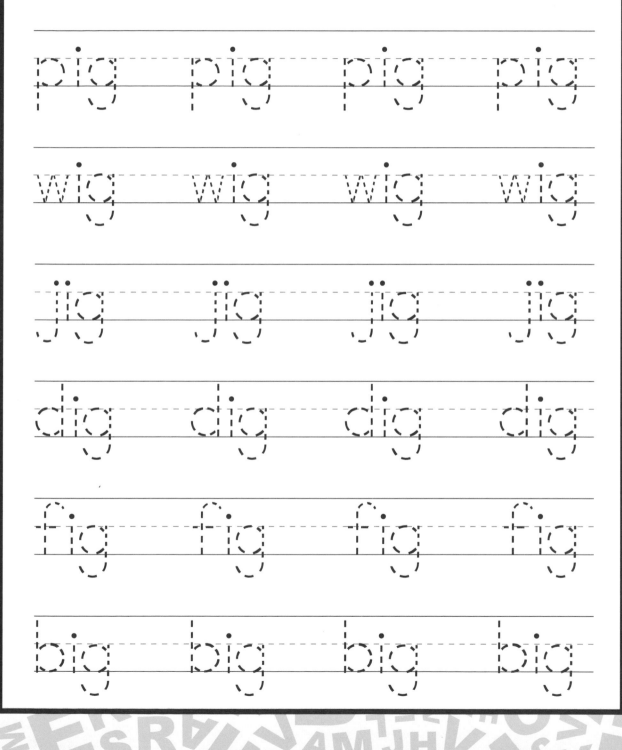

Activity Time

Find and circle the words from the **-ig** word family.

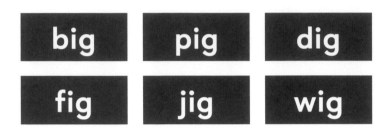

V J I N F

B I G O I

W G P I G

I D I G G

G B P W B

The Map

SKILL FOCUS:
-ap word family

Look! A map!

Go find a gap.

Now find a red cap.

Here is the cap.

Give it a rap.

Zap! Here it is!

Activity Time

Say the words. Then trace the words.

map map map map

gap gap gap gap

cap cap cap cap

cap cap cap cap

rap rap rap rap

zap zap zap zap

Find the words from the **-ap** word family. Circle each one.

look

gap

here

find

is

now

red

cap

give

a

the

rap

it

zap

map

Where Is Mutt?

SKILL FOCUS:

-ut word family

This is Tut.

Tut looks for his dog, Mutt.

He goes in a hut.

He does not see Mutt.

But Tut finds a nut.

So he puts the nut in his gut!

LEARN TO READ

Activity Time

Say the words. Then trace the words.

Tut Tut Tut Tut

Mutt Mutt Mutt

hut hut hut hut

but but but but

nut nut nut nut

gut gut gut gut

Activity Time

Circle the words from the **-ut** word family.

 Tut

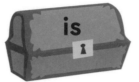 is

 the

 gut

 but

 in

 see

 the

 Mutt

 hut

 did

 gut

Ken and Jen

SKILL FOCUS:
-en word family

There is Ken.

Ken has a pen.

This is Ken's hen, Jen.

"Jen, may I have ten?" asks Ken.

Jen wants the pen.

Ken has ten.

Activity Time

Say the words. Then trace the words.

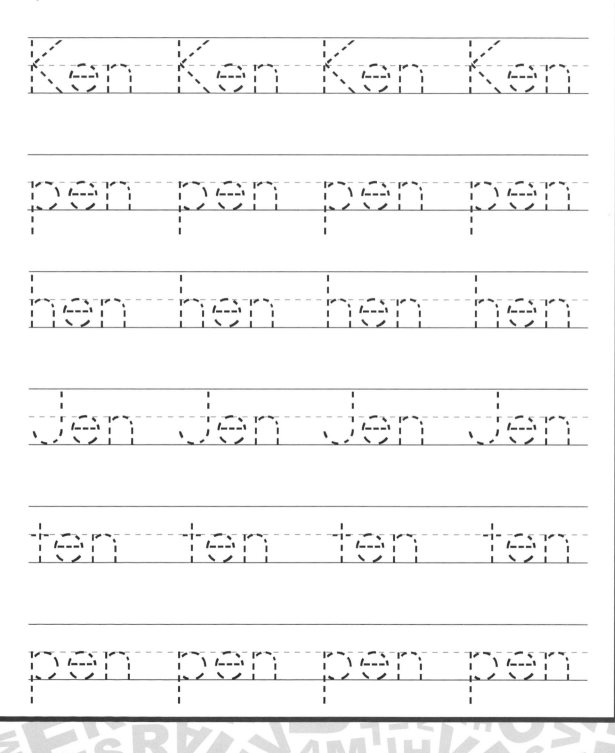

Ken Ken Ken Ken

pen pen pen pen

hen hen hen hen

Jen Jen Jen Jen

ten ten ten ten

pen pen pen pen

Find the words from the **-en** word family. Circle each one.

Ken

this

is

pen

will

the

hen

Jen

make

asks

to

has

ten

the

wants

Kit's Pit

SKILL FOCUS:
-it word family

Kit digs a pit.

She does not fit in it.

LEARN TO READ

Kit digs a bit more.

Kit fits!

They all fit in the pit.

And now the pit is lit!

Activity Time

Say the words. Then trace the words.

Activity Time

Complete the maze. Color the circles that have words from the **–it** word family.

Kit	the	of	and	a	to
fit	pit	in	is	you	that
he	bit	fit	was	for	on
are	as	lit	Kit	with	his
they	I	at	bit	pit	be
this	have	from	or	fit	one
had	by	words	but	Kit	pit

Pat
the Rat

SKILL FOCUS:
-at word family

This is Pat the rat.

Pat sat on the mat.

The rat saw a cat—

—a very fat cat.

The cat sat.

Now Pat the rat is flat.

Say the words. Then trace the words.

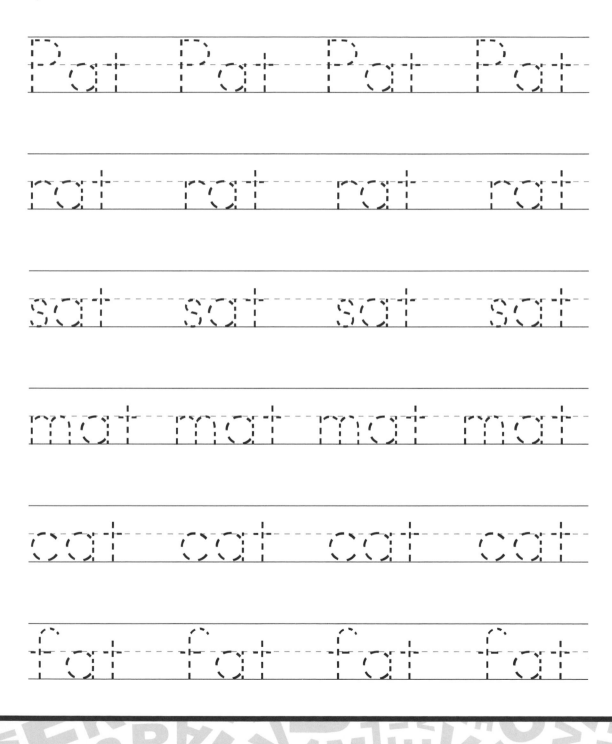

Pat Pat Pat Pat

rat rat rat rat

sat sat sat sat

mat mat mat mat

cat cat cat cat

fat fat fat fat

Activity Time

Complete the maze. Color the circles that have words from the **-at** word family.

rat	jig	the	jig	made	and
flat	cat	a	up	sit	sax
fax	Pat	box	Kit	pig	rap
lit	sat	fig	gap	this	bit
map	mat	top	each	he	can
fit	fat	sat	flat	mat	rat
see	tap	she	dig	cap	fat

Dad and Lad

SKILL FOCUS:
-ad word family
-ab word family

Lad and Dad nab a cab.

Lad gabs with Dad.

Dad and Lad go in the lab.

"Not bad," said Dad.

"Just a tad," said Lad.

Lad and Dad have fun at the lab!

Activity Time

Say the words. Then trace the words.

Lad Lad Lad Lad

Dad Dad Dad Dad

nab nab nab nab

cab cab cab cab

gab gab gab gab

bad bad bad bad

Activity Time

Find and circle the words from the **-ab** and **-ad** word families.

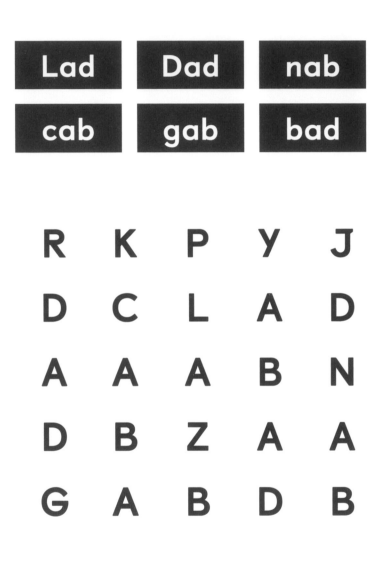

Lad	Dad	nab
cab	gab	bad

R K P Y J

D C L A D

A A A B N

D B Z A A

G A B D B

Jox
and Jax

SKILL FOCUS:
-ox word family
-ax word family

Jox is a fox.

Jox plays in a box.

Jax is a boy.

Jax plays the sax.

Jox and Jax need a big box.

Jax plays sax with Jox in the box.

Activity Time

Say the words. Then trace the words.

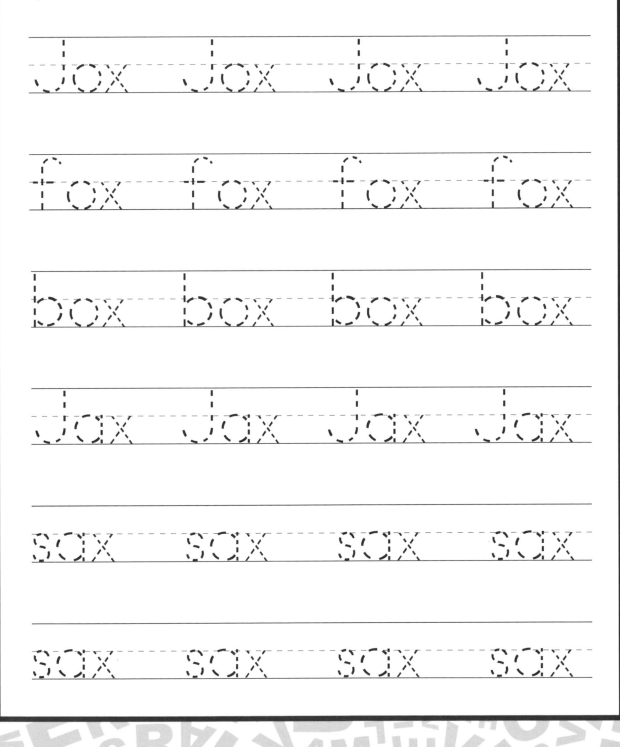

Jox Jox Jox Jox

fox fox fox fox

box box box box

Jax Jax Jax Jax

sax sax sax sax

sax sax sax sax

Activity Time

Circle the words from the **-OX** word family.

LEARN TO READ

Let's Go Up!

SKILL FOCUS:
-ip word family
-up word family

Let's go up!

Sip from the cup.

Here comes a dip!

Do not tip the cup!

Time is up! We go down.

Now let's zip up!

Activity Time

Say the words. Then trace the words.

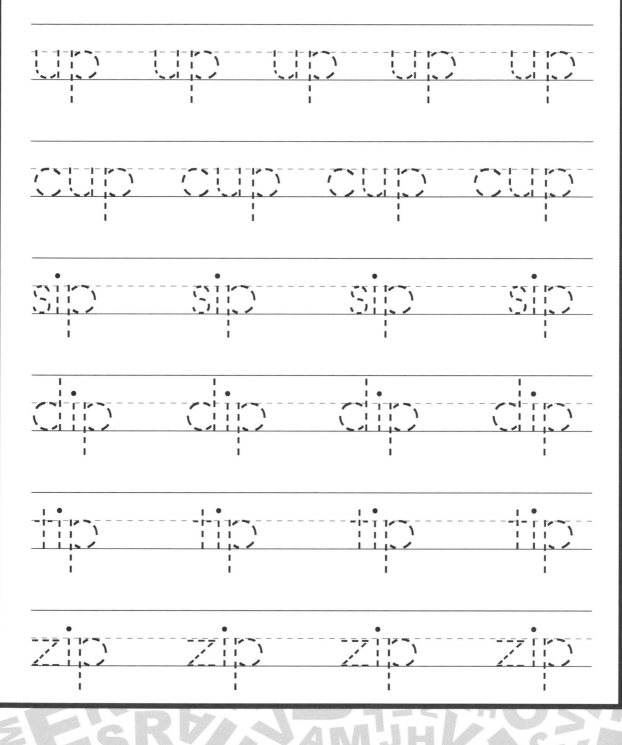

up up up up up

cup cup cup cup

sip sip sip sip

dip dip dip dip

tip tip tip tip

zip zip zip zip

Activity Time

Find and circle the words from the **-ip** and **-up** word families.

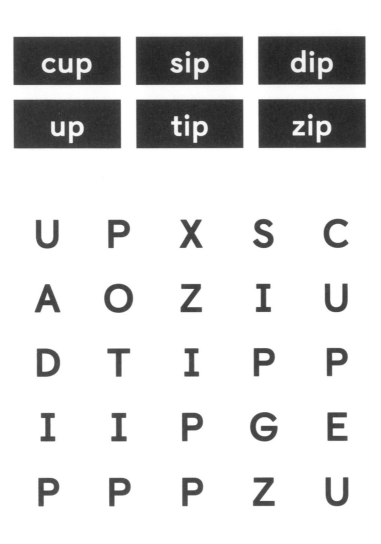

cup   sip   dip

up   tip   zip

U P X S C

A O Z I U

D T I P P

I I P G E

P P P Z U

Gum in the Sun

SKILL FOCUS:
-um word family
-un word family

Gum!

Gum in the sun.

LEARN TO READ

Here comes a drum!

Gum in my bun?

Help from Mum.

Gum is fun.

Activity Time

Say the words. Then trace the words.

gum gum gum gum

sun   sun   sun   sun

drum   drum   drum

bun bun bun bun

mum   mum   mum

fun fun fun fun

Find and circle the words from the **-um** and **-un** word families.

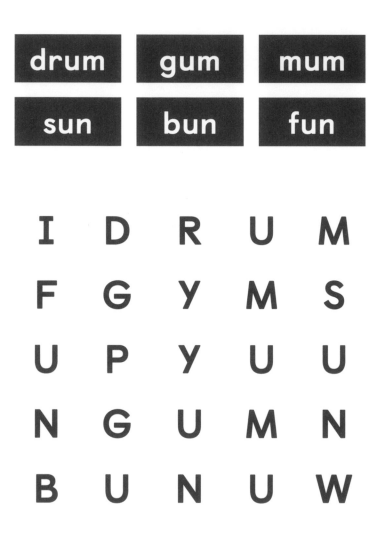

drum	gum	mum
sun	bun	fun

I D R U M

F G Y M S

U P Y U U

N G U M N

B U N U W

Rags

SKILL FOCUS:
-ag word family

This is my dog, Rags.

Rags and I play tag.

LEARN TO READ

Rags can wag, wag, wag.

What is in the bag, Rags?

Look! It's a flag!

Now I can wag, wag, wag!

Activity Time

Say the words. Then trace the words.

tag tag tag tag

wag wag wag wag

bag bag bag bag

flag flag flag

wag wag wag wag

Rags Rags Rags

Activity Time

Circle the words from the **-ag** word family.

 rag

 can

 tag

 drum

 cap

 Tim

 bag

 gum

 wag

 sun

 flag

 tip

Cub and Bug

SKILL FOCUS:
-ub word family
-ug word family

Cub goes to his club.

Cub looks for Bug.

Cub looks in the mug.

Where is Bug?

Bug is under the rug!

Bug gives Cub a little hug.

Activity Time

Say the words. Then trace the words.

Activity Time

Find and circle the words from the **-ub** and **-ug** word families.

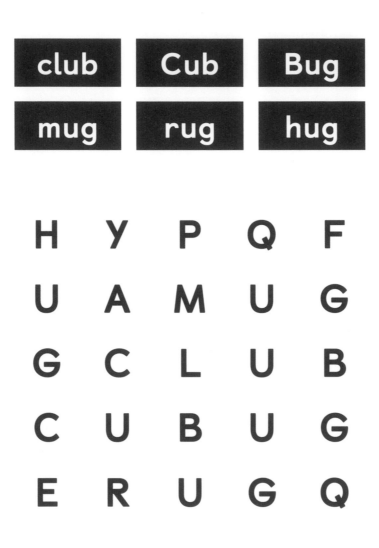

club   Cub   Bug

mug   rug   hug

H Y P Q F
U A M U G
G C L U B
C U B U G
E R U G Q

Rob's Job

SKILL FOCUS:
-ob word family

Rob has a job.

Bob gets a cob from Rob.

"Do you want a blob?" asks Rob.

"Yes, a big glob!" says Bob.

"Oh no!" Rob sobs.

Bob helps Rob get cob for the mob.

Activity Time

Say the words. Then trace the words.

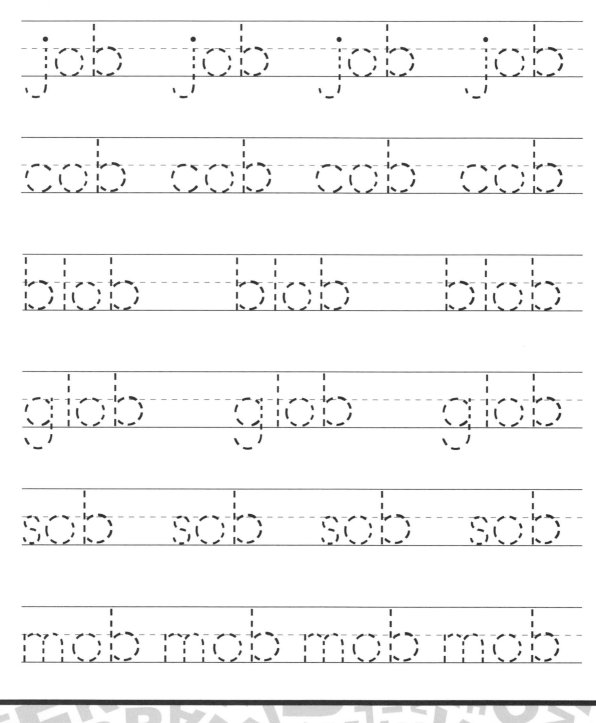

job job job job

cob cob cob cob

blob blob blob

glob glob glob

sob sob sob sob

mob mob mob mob

Activity Time

Complete the maze. Color the circles that have words from the **-ob** word family.

mob	what	all	were	we	when
blob	sun	can	said	there	use
cob	blob	sag	pit	which	she
do	job	how	their	tag	what
all	Rob	were	we	rip	your
can	cob	said	there	rid	an
each	sob	job	mob	glob	Bob

Let's Sled

SKILL FOCUS:
-ed word family

Ned had a red sled.

Ned led Ted up the hill.

Ned and Ted fled down the hill.

Ted sped past Ned.

Ted won!

Now Ned has to make the beds.

LEARN TO READ

Activity Time

Say the words. Then trace the words.

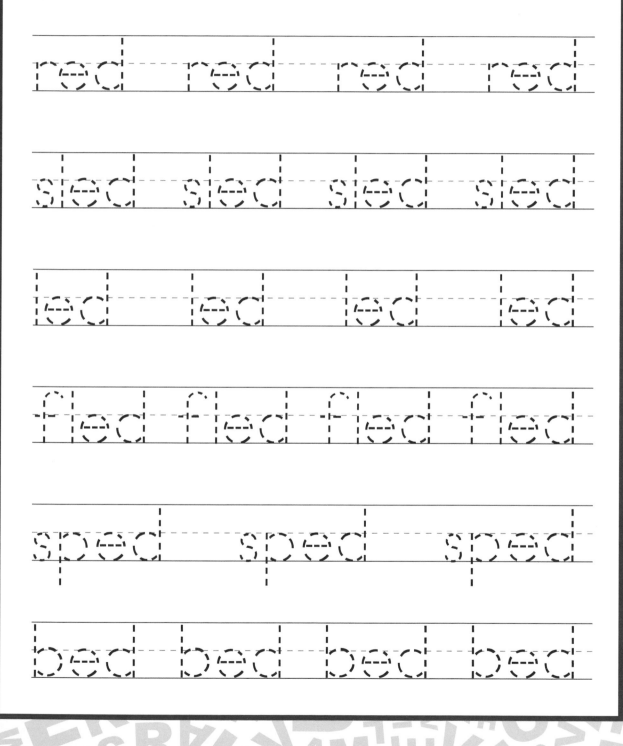

red red red red

sled sled sled sled

led led led led

fled fled fled fled

sped sped sped

bed bed bed bed

Activity Time

Find the words from the **-ed** word family. Circle each one.

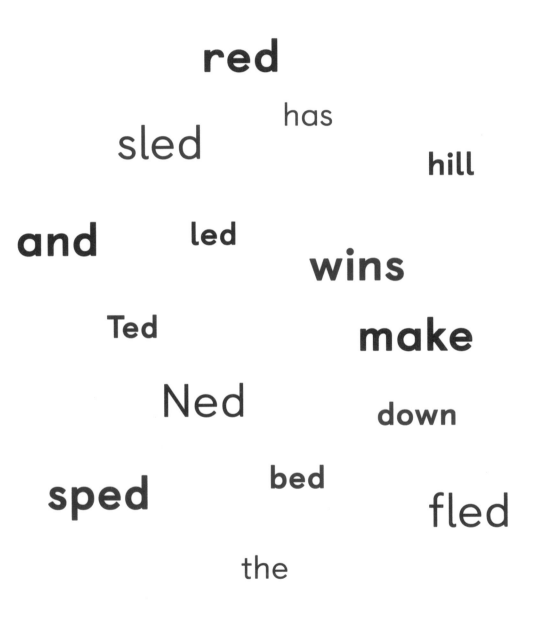

red

has

sled

hill

and

led

wins

Ted

make

Ned

down

sped

bed

fled

the

Dot's Spots

SKILL FOCUS:
-ot word family

Dot is a tot.

She has lots of spots.

Dot plays with a bot.

She likes to trot.

But when Dot gets hot . . .

. . . she sits on my cot.

Activity Time

Say the words. Then trace the words.

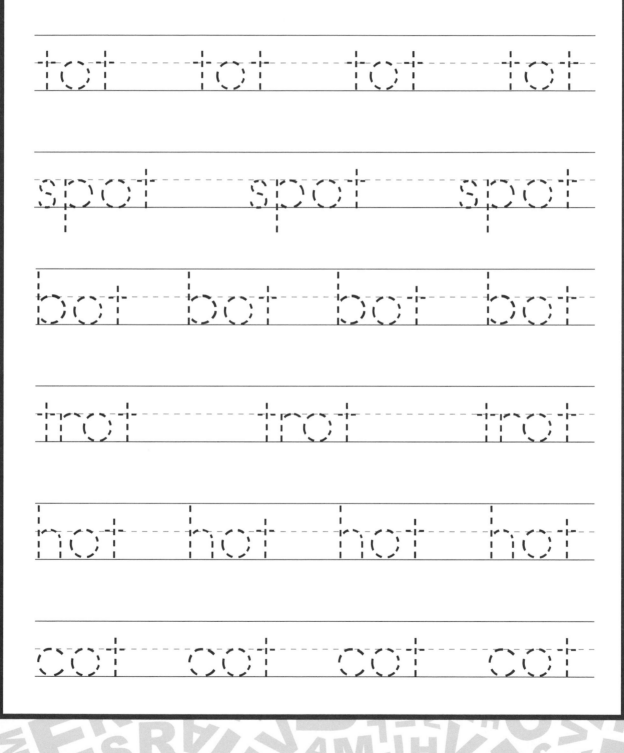

tot   tot   tot   tot

spot   spot   spot

bot   bot   bot   bot

trot   trot   trot

hot   hot   hot   hot

cot   cot   cot   cot

Activity Time

Circle the words from the **-ot** word family.

 dot

 tot

spot

 cub

 bot

hen

 hot

 cot

rub

 mop

 cap

 tub

At the Bog

SKILL FOCUS:
-og word family

Grog was a frog.

He lived by a bog.

Grog went for a jog.

He sat on a log.

Then he looked at the fog . . .

. . . with Slog the hog.

Activity Time

Say the words. Then trace the words.

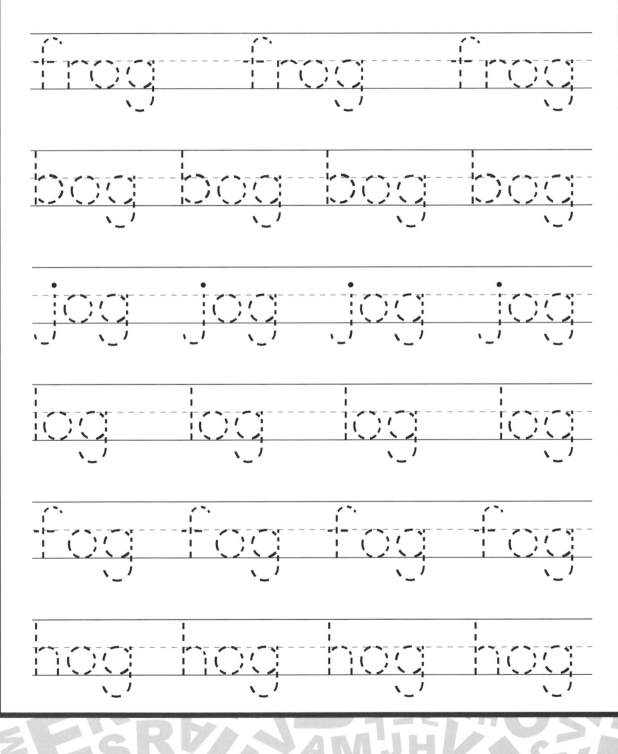

Activity Time

Complete the maze. Color the circles that have words from the **-og** word family.

Grog	frog	log	but	Ken	map
the	she	bog	a	pen	by
trap	jig	jog	fog	pig	we
sap	when	wig	log	hog	see
man	Jen	by	words	Slog	frog
are	they	I	have	but	hog
Ken	map	the	she	a	fog

Oh, Pops!

SKILL FOCUS:

-op word family

Pops mops.

Pops drops.

Pops hops.

Pops flops.

Pops plops!

Pops is tops!

Activity Time

Say the words. Then trace the words.

mop mop mop mop

hop hop hop hop

top top top top

flop flop flop

plop plop plop

drop drop drop

Activity Time

Find the words from the **-op** word family. Circle each one.

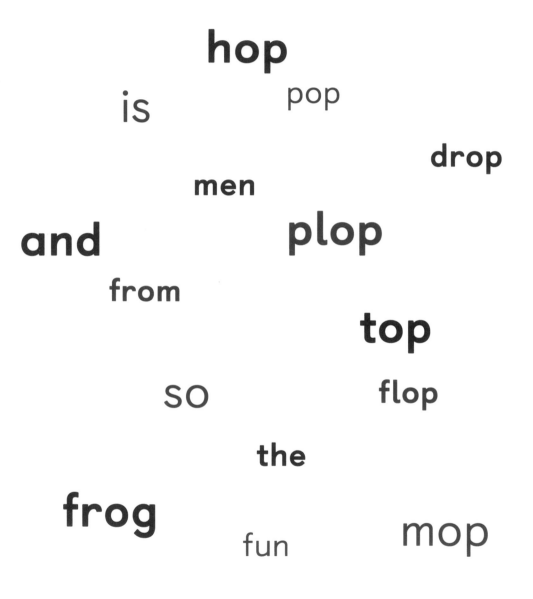

hop

is

pop

drop

men

plop

and

from

top

so

flop

the

frog

fun

mop

Good Luck Duck

SKILL FOCUS:
-uck word family

Look at that duck!

The duck snuck in the truck.

There goes the duck in the truck!

The truck is in the muck.

Yuck!

We are in luck!

LEARN TO READ

Activity Time

Say the words. Then trace the words.

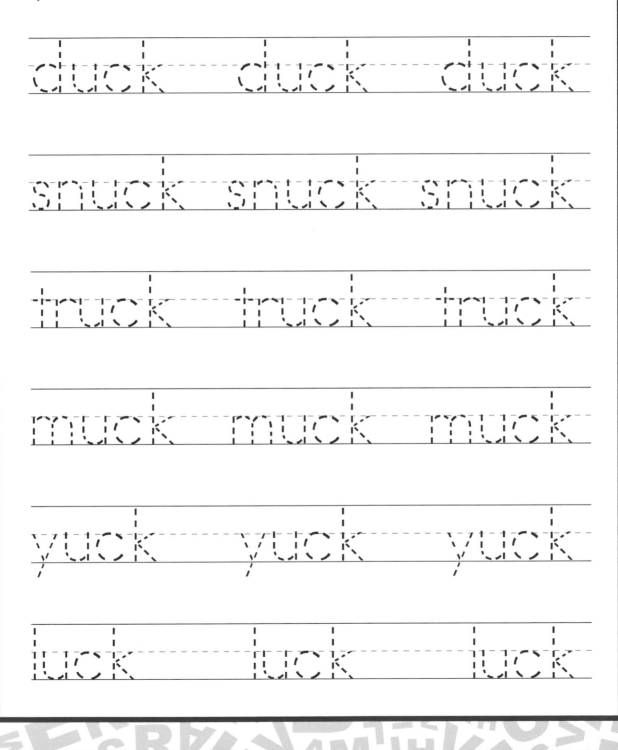

duck   duck   duck

snuck   snuck   snuck

truck   truck   truck

muck   muck   muck

yuck   yuck   yuck

luck   luck   luck

Activity Time

Find and circle the words from the **-uck** word family.

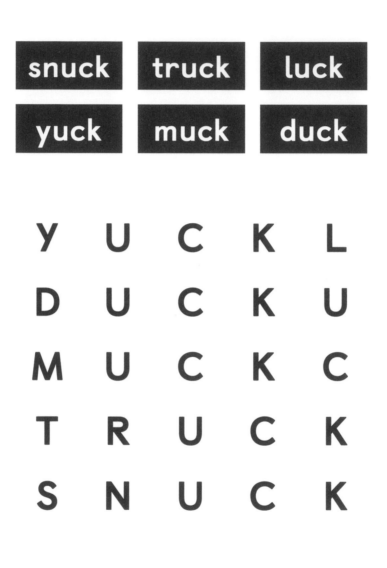

snuck   truck   luck

yuck   muck   duck

Y U C K L
D U C K U
M U C K C
T R U C K
S N U C K

The Track

SKILL FOCUS:
-ack word family

Crack!

There goes Jack!

They run on the black track.

FINISH

Jack is in front of the pack!

Now Jack wants a snack.

They all need a snack!

Activity Time

Say the words. Then trace the words.

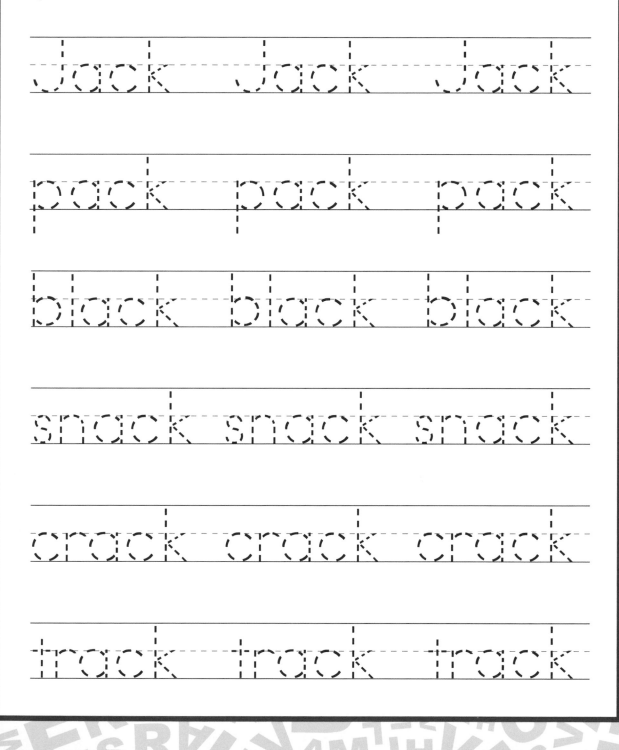

Jack   Jack   Jack

pack   pack   pack

black   black   black

snack   snack   snack

crack   crack   crack

track   track   track

Activity Time

Color the words from the **-ack** word family.

truck

track

said

Jack

duck

black

muck

snack

pack

trick

day

crack

Peck, Peck, Peck!

SKILL FOCUS:
-eck word family

I am on the deck.

Peck, peck, peck!

I stop to check.

They left some specks.

Look at all the flecks.

I can fix the wreck.

LEARN TO READ

Activity Time

Say the words. Then trace the words.

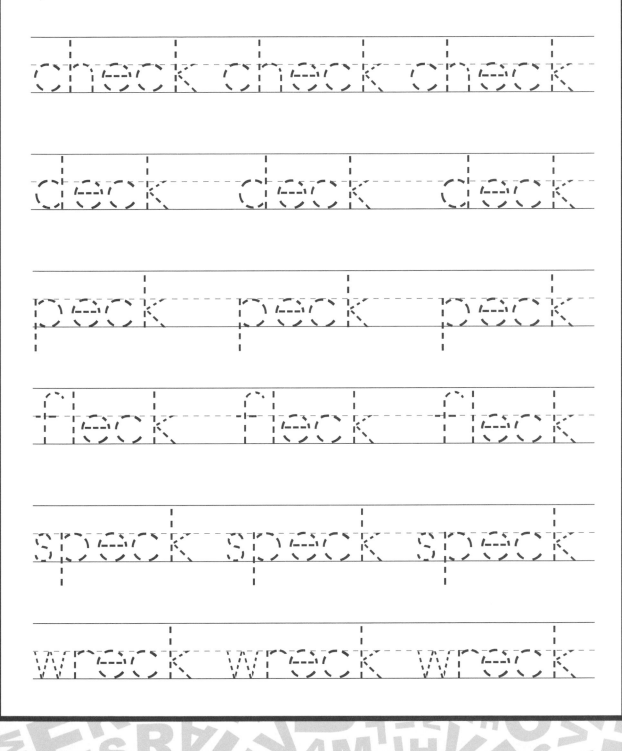

check check check

deck   deck   deck

peck   peck   peck

fleck   fleck   fleck

speck speck speck

wreck wreck wreck

Find the words from the **-eck** word family. Circle each one.

peck

left

pack

deck

fleck

sack

wreck

tack

crack

speck

the neck

fix

back

check

I Can Do Tricks!

SKILL FOCUS:

-ick word family

I can do a trick.

Pick a stick.

Click, click, click!

Is this your stick?

Lick it, quick!

That was a slick trick.

Activity Time

Say the words. Then trace the words.

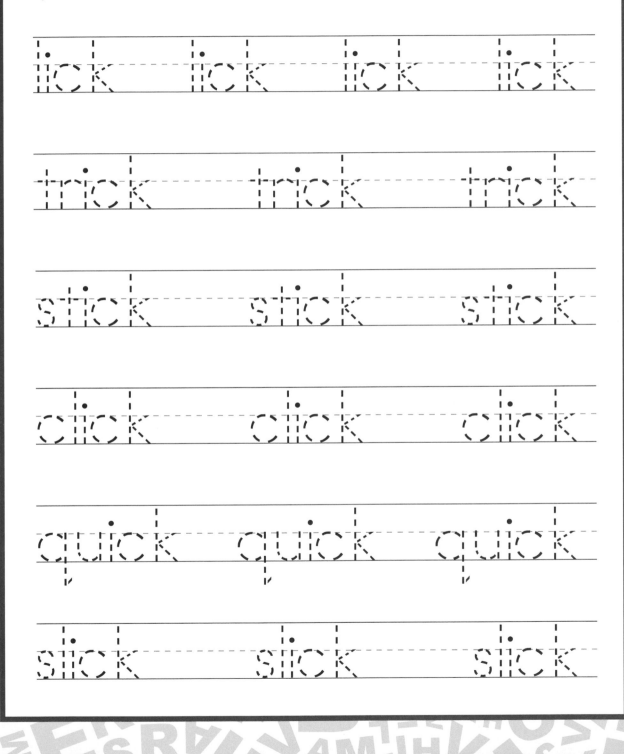

lick   lick   lick   lick

trick   trick   trick

stick   stick   stick

click   click   click

quick   quick   quick

slick   slick   slick

Complete the maze. Color the circles that have words from the **-ick** word family.

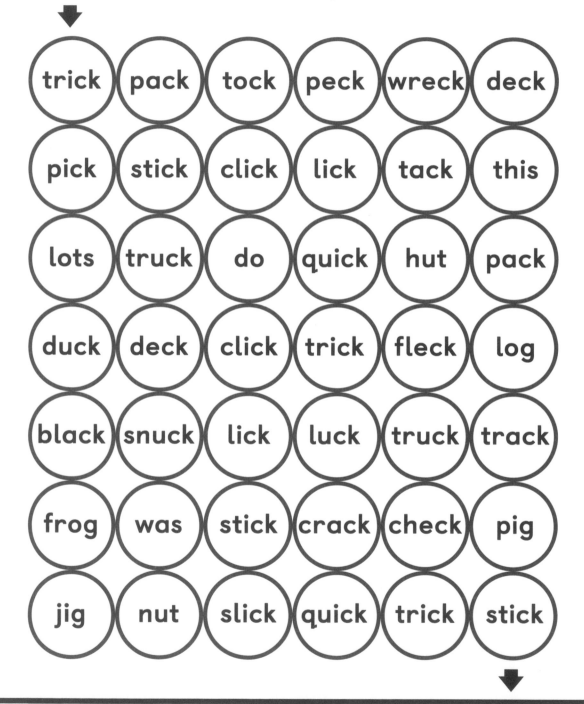

trick	pack	tock	peck	wreck	deck
pick	stick	click	lick	tack	this
lots	truck	do	quick	hut	pack
duck	deck	click	trick	fleck	log
black	snuck	lick	luck	truck	track
frog	was	stick	crack	check	pig
jig	nut	slick	quick	trick	stick

The Sock

SKILL FOCUS:
-ock word family

Do you see my other sock?

Could it be under a rock?

LEARN TO READ

Could it be by the clock?

Could it be in Mom's smock?

Tick tock, tick tock. I need that sock!

Oh, there is my sock!

Activity Time

Say the words. Then trace the words.

Activity Time

Find and circle the words from the **-ock** word family.

clock   rock   smock

sock   tock

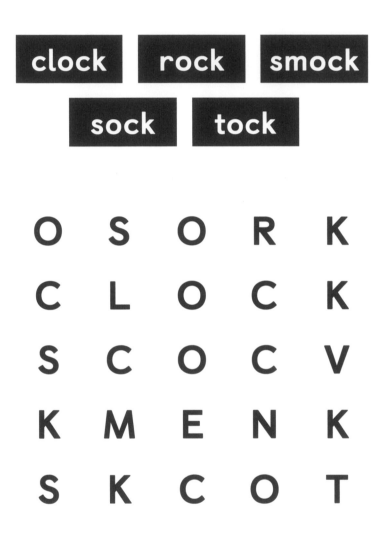

O S O R K

C L O C K

S C O C V

K M E N K

S K C O T

Swim, Swim, Swim!

SKILL FOCUS:
-im word family
-in word family

We put on our fins.

Let's jump in!

We see Min and Tim.

They can do a spin.

We all spin and grin.

We love to swim!

Activity Time

Say the words. Then trace the words.

Activity Time

Circle the words from the **-in** word family.

 Min  dim  spin

 Tim  swim  rim

 fin  grin  trim

 in  him  Jim

The Web

SKILL FOCUS:
-eb word family
-eg word family

Peg and Meg were going fast.

"Look out for the web!" said Deb.

But Meg went in the web.

"My leg is stuck," said Meg.

"Help!" Peg begged.

"So long, web," said Deb.

LEARN TO READ

Activity Time

Say the words. Then trace the words.

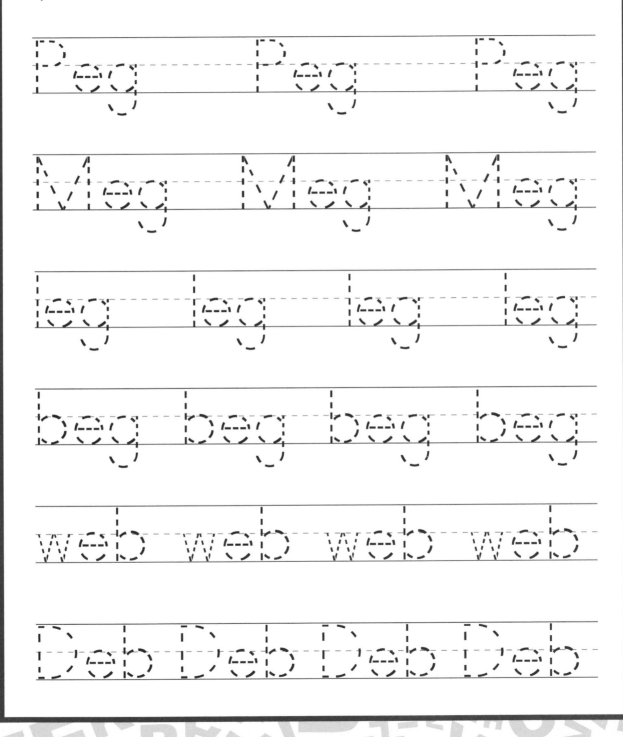

Activity Time

Complete the maze. Color the circles that have
words from the **-eb** and **-eg** word families.

Deb	fat	in	look	rat	they
web	Meg	fat	the	fox	help
Jim	leg	beg	kit	Tim	bot
tot	cat	web	leg	box	tick
sock	fit	pen	Meg	Peg	bat
fox	jig	win	sat	beg	Deb
Min	pit	trot	tock	bit	web

Index

· ·

About the Author

Laurin Brainard, M.Ed., is the founder of www.theprimarybrain.com. Through her blog, Laurin shares preschool ideas, fun activities, crafts, and elementary teaching tips. Laurin is a first-grade teacher, mom to two preschoolers, and the curriculum designer for The Primary Brain. When she isn't teaching or designing curriculum, Laurin enjoys playing and making memories with her family.

About the Illustrator

Lizzy Doyle is a designer, illustrator, and author living in New Jersey. She graduated from the Fashion Institute of Technology in 2012 with a degree in graphic design. Lizzy began her career in publishing designing books, craft kits, and specialty toys. She is now the creator and owner of Lizzy Dee Studio where she creates cute characters, patterns for apparel and decor, and illustrations for licensing.